Can You

by Althea

Illustrated by Ljiljana Rylands

Published by Dinosaur Publications

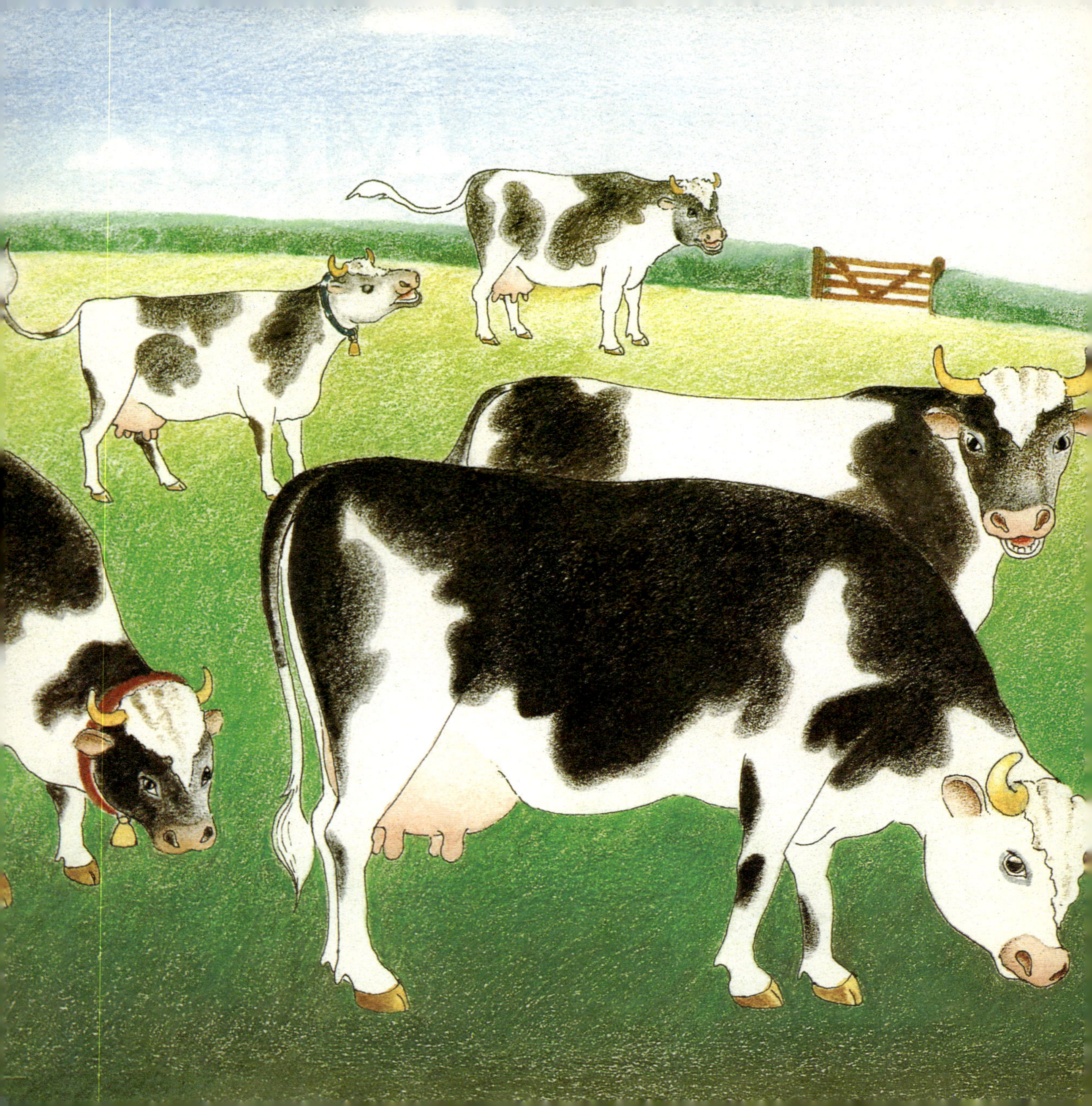

Can you moo like the cows munching grass in the fields?

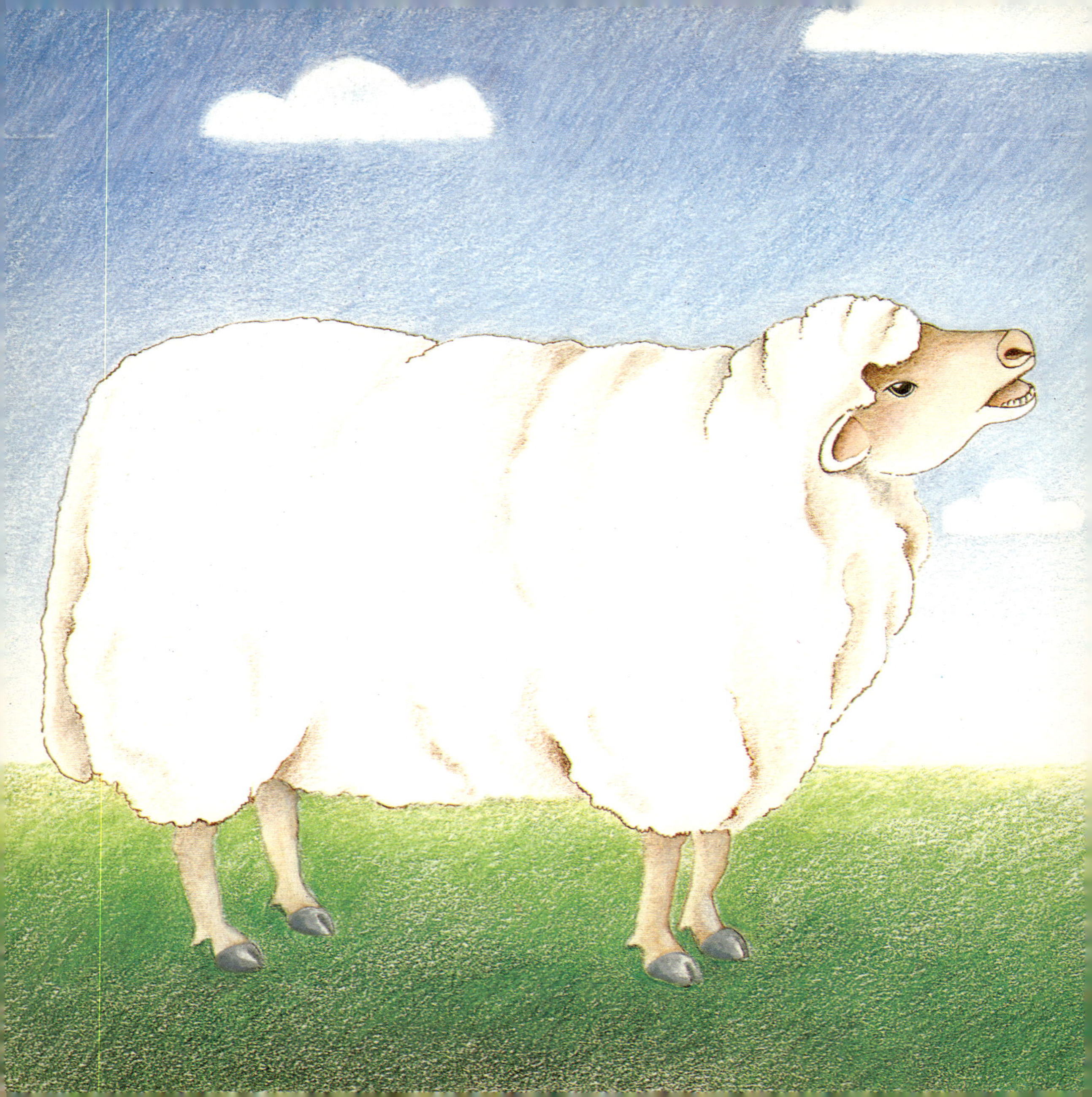

Can you baah like the sheep
or bleat like the baby lambs?

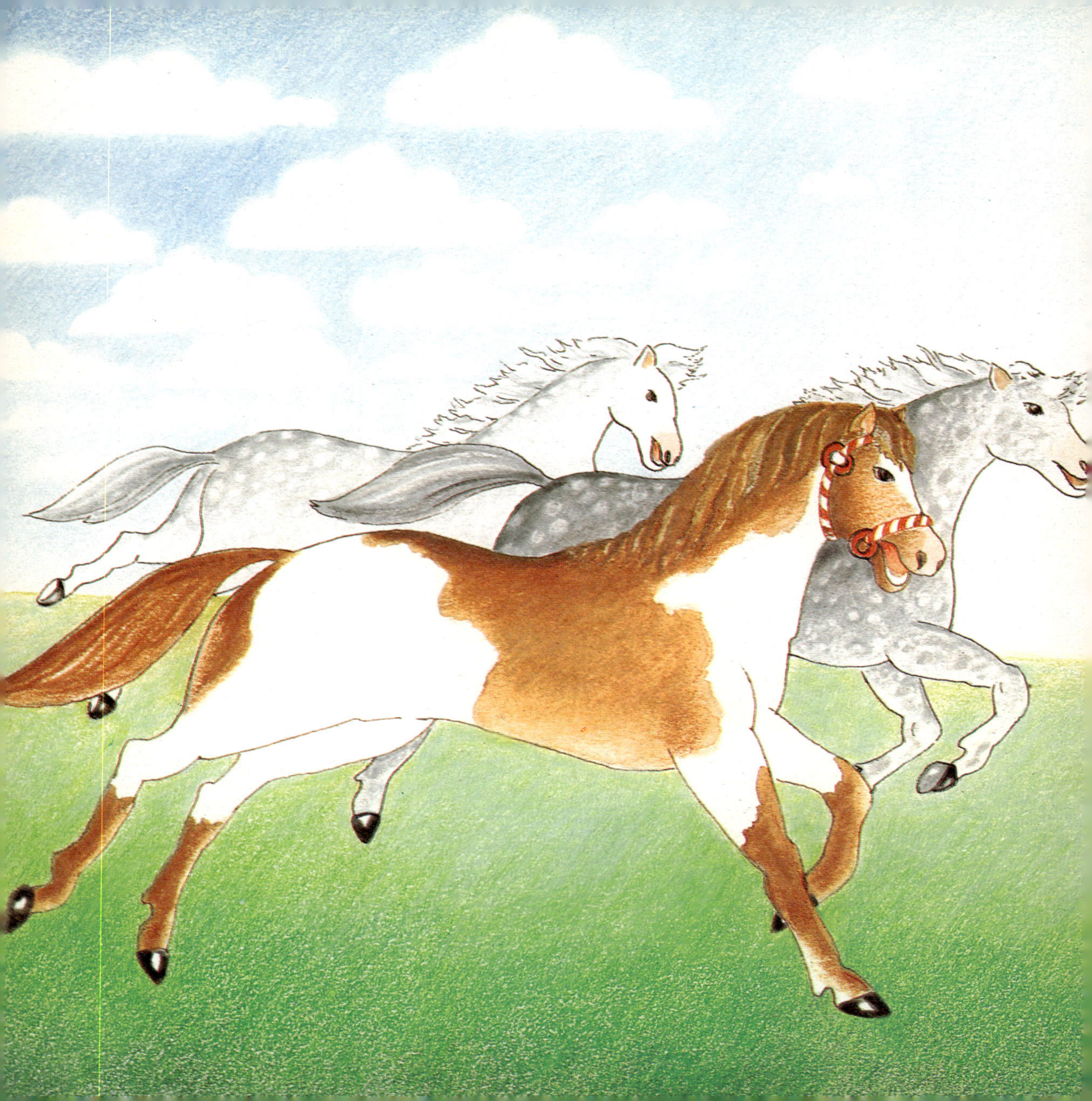

Can you neigh like the horses
as they gallop away?

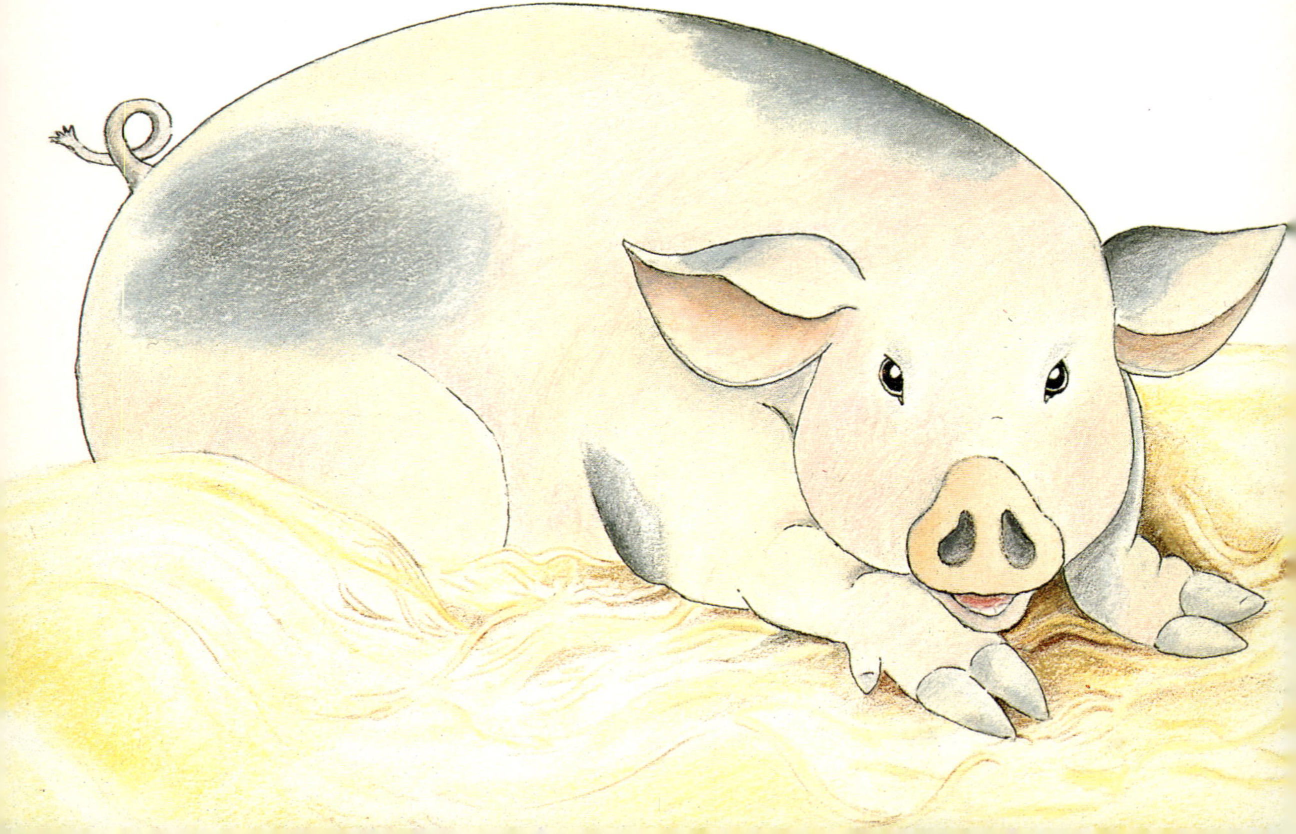

Can you grunt like the pig
snuffling in her sty?

Can you quack like the ducks swimming in the pond?

Can you hiss like the geese
as they stretch out their long necks?

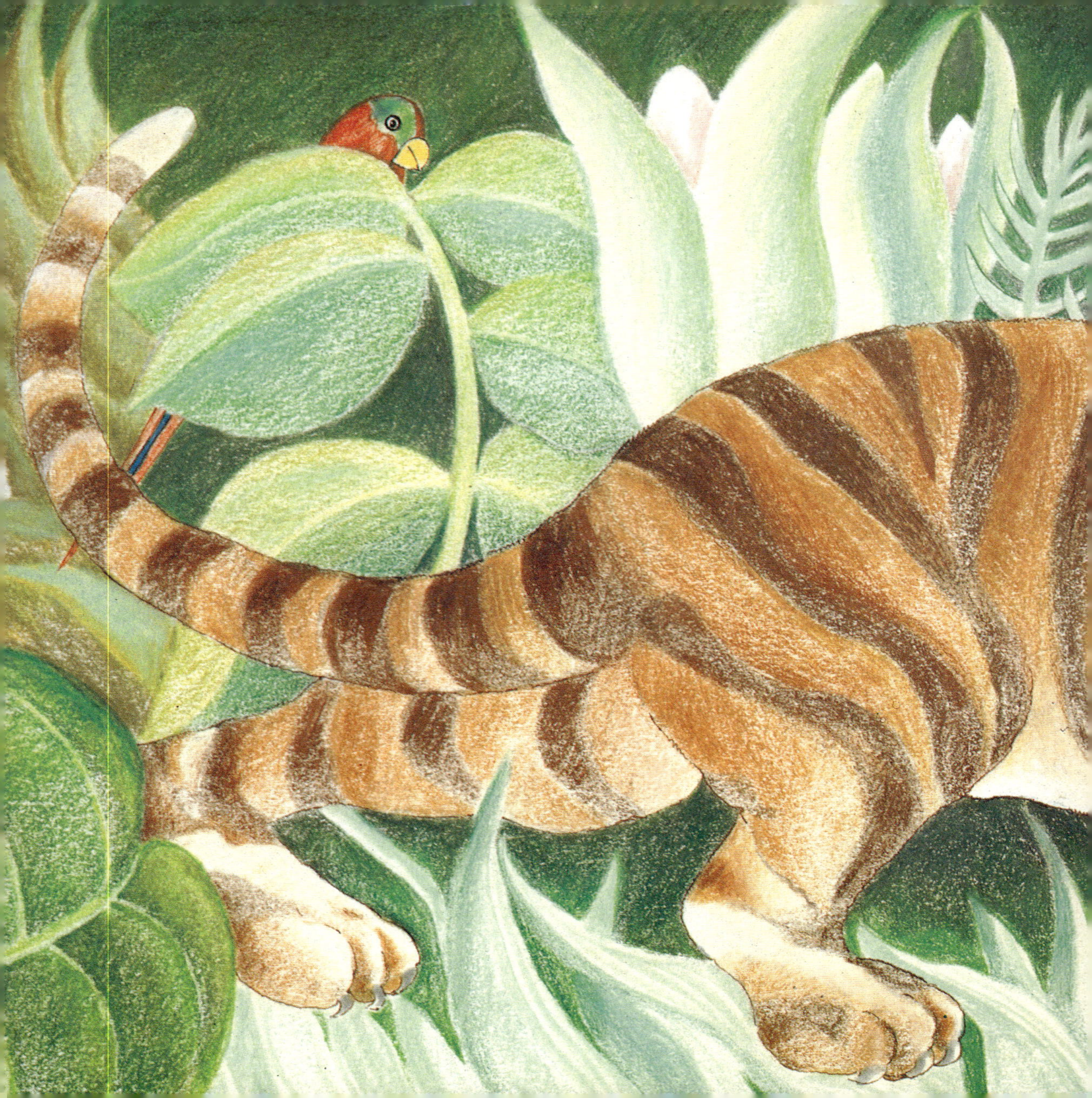

Can you roar like the tiger prowling through the jungle?

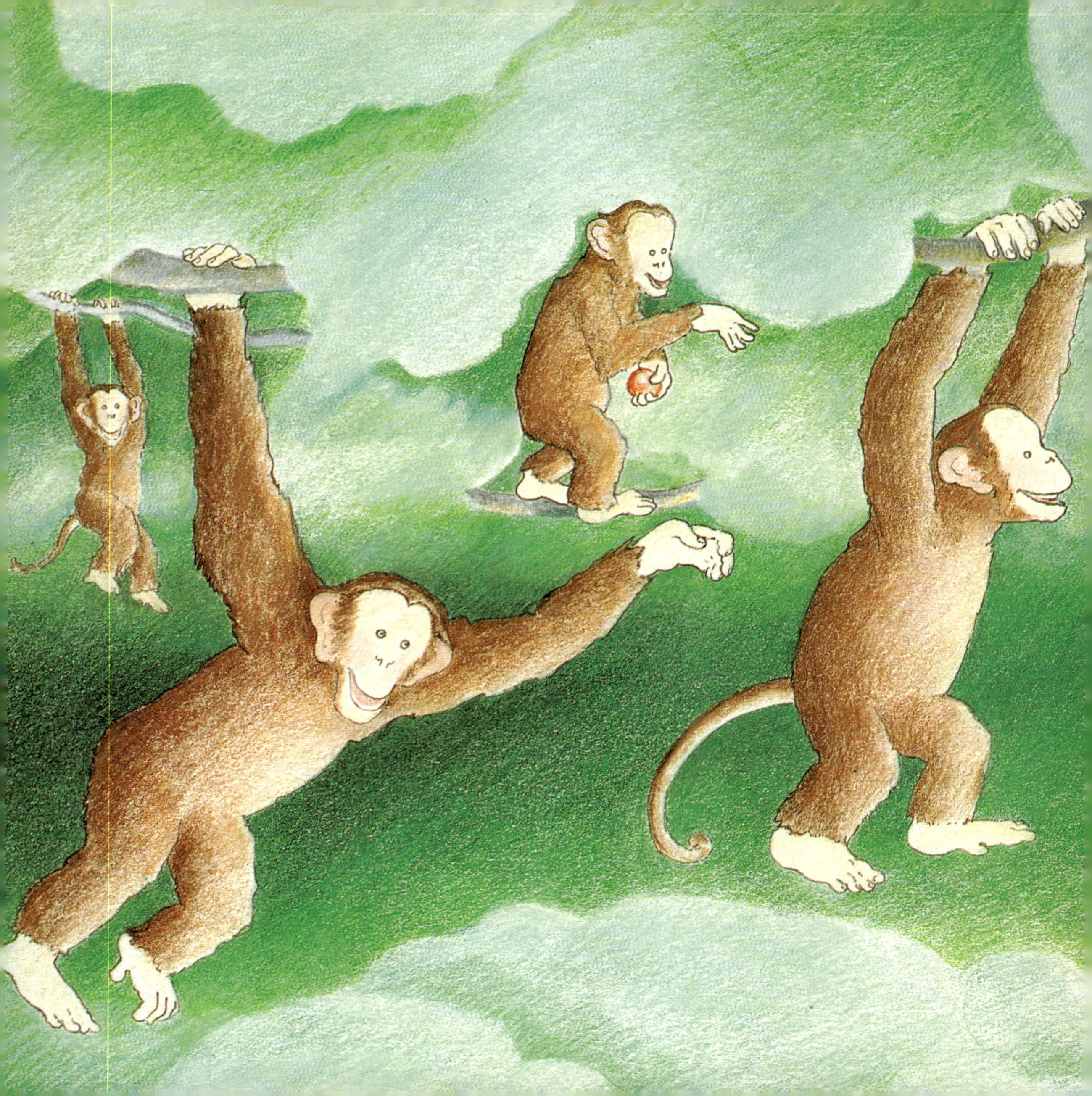

Can you chatter like the monkeys swinging through the trees?

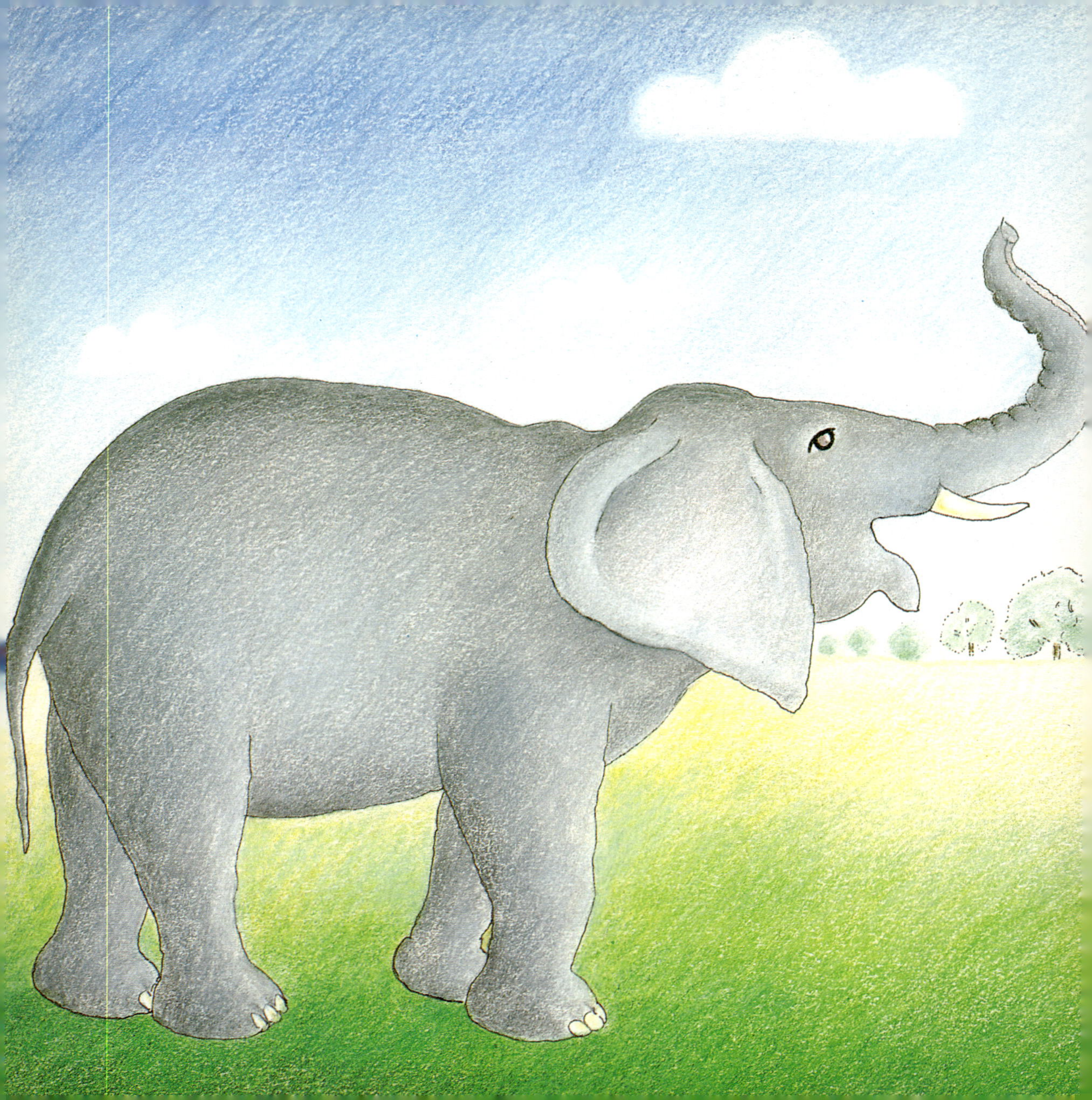

Can you trumpet like the elephant calling to her child?

Can you twit-twoo like the owl
as he flies through the night?

Can you squeak like the mouse running to hide?

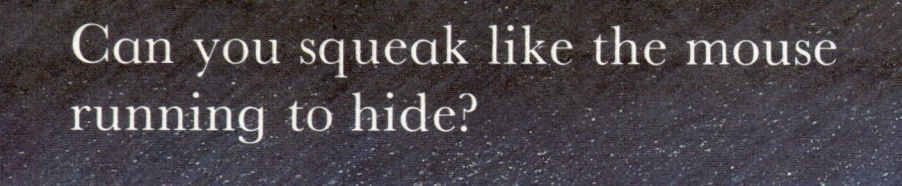

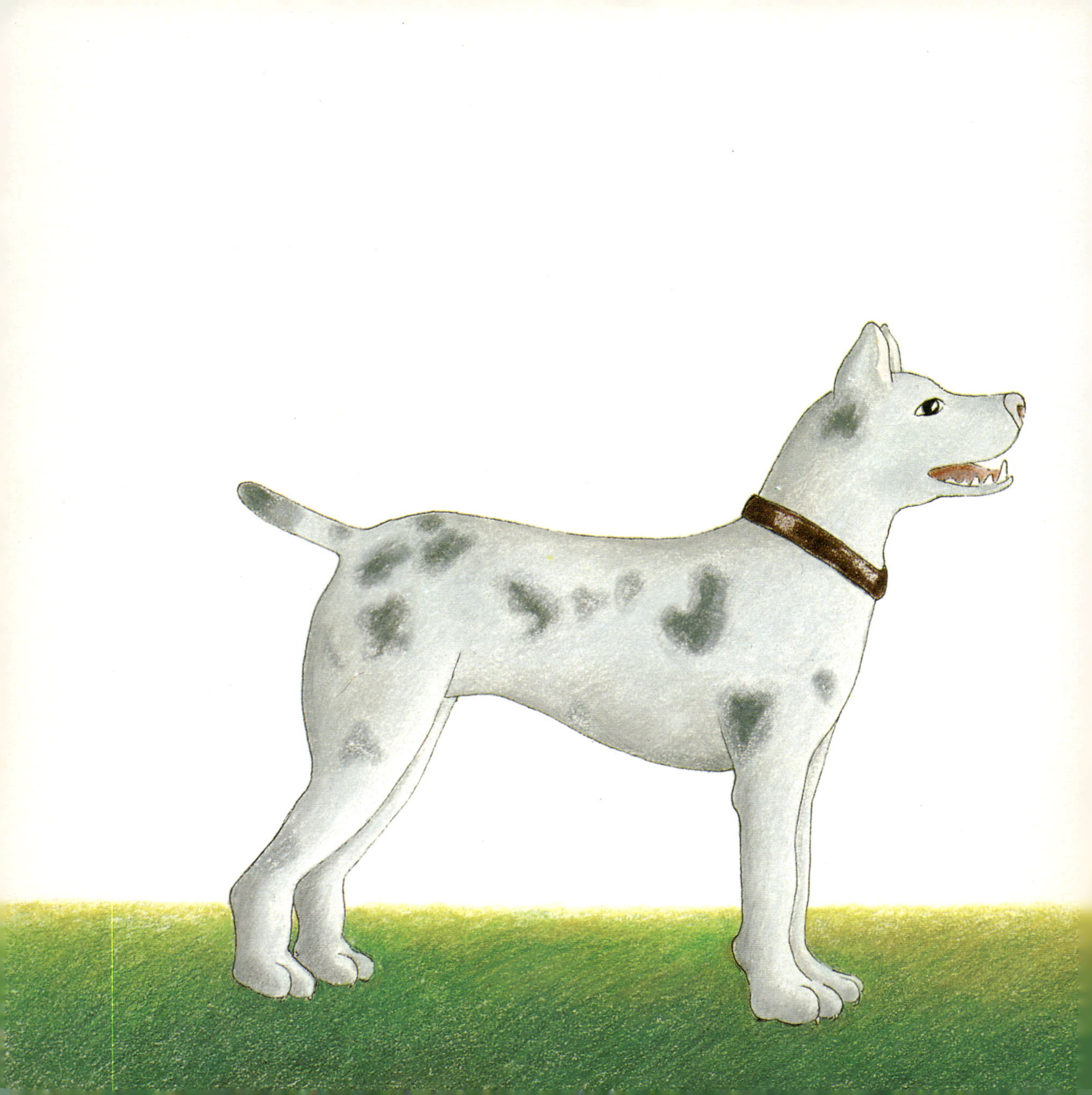

Can you bark and growl
like the dog on guard?

Can you purr like this contented cat?

He will miaow when he is hungry.
Can you?